Wedding ~~Bells~~

Cause for Thanksgiving

Min Margaret O Odeleye

Copyright

Copyright 2022 **Wedding Bells: Cause for Thanksgiving -** By Margaret O Odeleye

All rights reserved. No part of this publication may be reproduced, distributed, or transmitted in any form, or by any means, including photocopying, recording or other electronic or mechanical methods, without prior written permission from the author and publisher.

Unless otherwise stated, Bible references are taken from the New King James Version®. Copyright © 1982 by Thomas Nelson. Used by permission. All rights reserved.

Book editing and formatting by: Dr Jacqueline Samuels

Visit: https://tinyurl.com/AuthorJNSamuels

Cover Design by https://serve-and-thrive-academy.thinkific.com/

Let's connect at **fol58@outlook.com**

For other books by the author visit:

https://www.amazon.co.uk/Margaret-Odeleye/e/B0984R47TW/

ISBN: 9798374235142

Dedication

I want to honour our great God and Creator who has given us the gift of abundant life through His Son Jesus Christ.

To the three generations of family members who have touched my life:

My late father, Mr Joseph T. Olufayo and mother, Mrs Alice Olufayo who first taught me the principles of Christ.

My husband, Barrister I. A. Odeleye who following in my parents' footsteps has been a constant support through this journey of life.

My children, Gideon, Esther and Blessing who have motivated me to pray and are now incredible answers to my relentless intercession.

Contents

Copyright	iii
Dedication	iv
Endorsements	vii
Foreword	xi
Acknowledgements	xiii
Introduction	xvi
Chapter One: The Origin of Marriage	1
Chapter Two: God's Purpose for Marriage	7
Preparation for growth in maturity	8
Chapter Three: Creating a Successful Marriage	13
Quiz!	17
Chapter Four: Three Pillars of Marriage	22
1st Pillar: Your identity	23
2nd Pillar: Your literature	25
3rd Pillar: Your conduct and wardrobe (while single)	26
Chapter Five: 5 Benefits of Marriage	30
Chapter Six: Challenges Within Marriages	34
Challenge One: Differences in personality	35
Challenge Two: Issues with in-laws	37
Challenge Three: Lack of finances	38
Challenge Four: Delay in the promise of having children	38
Chapter Seven: Marriage Advice	43
Chapter Eight: Redemption in Christ	49
About the Author	54
Other Books by the Author	55

Endorsements

The word *marriage* dates to the creation of man and woman. After God created Adam, He made Eve and said it is not good for man to be alone. This wonderful book starts off by reminding us first and foremost that marriage is a God idea, therefore it's a good idea.

I love the unwavering stance that marriage is good and comes with many benefits, some of which are listed in this book. The author argues that the success of a good marriage is proportional to the foundation, preparation, and commitment that two people have towards each other daily.

This is a must read for everyone including singles, intending couples, couples starting their journey in marriage, even couples who have been married for years. As many married couples know, in marriage every day is a school day with lots to learn. I wish I had discovered some of the nuggets this book reveals before I got married. However, as a wife I am now able to apply many of the tips the author has shared for a sweeter marriage.

I believe you won't regret buying this book for yourself, a friend or family member.

This gem can be used for personal study, as a reading resource for couples, and in marriage counselling sessions. The author also provides a great tool for salvation by introducing the reader to Christ, the Author and Creator of marriage.

Get stuck in and see for yourself!

Dr Esther Odeleye

This book is a must read for anyone curious and aspiring to marry, couples looking to refresh their knowledge on how to cultivate and get their marriage on track will benefit immensely from reading this book and using it as a reference book from time to time.

Wedding Bells lays a solid foundation for building a godly marriage. It captures beautifully and accurately the true meaning and essence of marriage and gives clear and actionable roadmap for achieving marital bliss. I highly recommend it.

Pastor Frank Abu

Senior Pastor, The Redeemed Christian Church of God Living Word Liberation Centre, Southampton

The 'Cause for Thanksgiving' appears to be superfluent in many aspects of our lives and is especially true in dominant areas such as our personal growth and celebrated successes. However, the popularity of the marriage institution is somehow forgotten as a call to action where the area of thanksgiving is concerned.

In her book Wedding Bells: Cause for Thanksgiving Minister Margaret has resurrected the need to celebrate God's original idea concerning the union between a man and a woman.

She has carefully summoned the reader to change their subjective views about marriage and instead embrace God's divine plan for the marriage institution.

Wedding Bells: Cause for Thanksgiving will enlighten your understanding about the purpose of marriage, consolidated by the pillars that will support a successful marriage.

The first pillar of marriage - Identity - the author's discussion will erase any self-doubt and help to transform your true self-image to embody that of Jesus Christ.

This book settles the foundation for anyone planning to get married and seeks to empower those already married to continue to embrace the sacredness of companionship and love to be experienced in marriage.

I have known Minister Margaret for two decades and she has inspired my life tremendously. She is a credible author, and her literature are justified by a lifestyle of integrity. The author herself has modelled these said values in another dynamic book, *Debt of Gratitude*, truly inspired by the Holy Spirit. It will captivate your mind to think on a brand-new level.

Minister Samantha Mayers
NTCG High Wycombe
LLM Legal Practice Solicitor | LLB (Hons)

Foreword

Marriage was God's idea which began in the Garden of Eden. We see it throughout the Bible. Since Jesus affirmed it during His ministry on earth, we need to take marriage seriously.

Unfortunately, marriage is less popular than ever in our society today. Divorce rates are high among those who do marry but many never reach that stage. The world tells us that relationships are temporary and can be disposed of whenever we so desire.

Therefore, it is vital to wrestle with what the Scriptures have to say about marriage. It is also important to learn from the experience of those who have entered this intimate union of man and woman.

I pray that what Minister Margaret has written will help you to consider what the Lord has to say to you concerning marriage. Whether you are approaching it for the first time or have been married for decades, we all have more to learn about marriage.

The Bible sets an incredibly high standard for what love is in 1 Corinthians 13.4-8:

"Love suffers long and is kind; love does not envy; love does not parade itself, is not puffed up; does not behave rudely, does not seek its own, is not (easily) provoked, thinks no evil; does not rejoice in iniquity, but rejoices in the truth; bears all things, believes all things, hopes all things, endures all things. Love never fails."
(Edit in bracket mine)

If only we all had that kind of love all the time. May your marriage express more and more of this godly love in the years to come.

Mr Kent Anderson

British Director of European Christian Mission

Acknowledgements

Deepest gratitude goes to my dear husband Barrister I. A. Odeleye for your relentless encouragement to follow my calling.

My daughter Dr Esther Odeleye, I am grateful for your creative support.

Minister Samantha Mayers, my learned friend, thank you for your editorial input.

Special thanks to Mr Kent Anderson for making time from his busy schedule as British Director of European Christian Mission to write the foreword. God bless you.

Bishop Malcolm Cummins, Aldershot District Overseer of The New Testament Church of God: deepest gratitude for your encouragement, guidance and support.

Pastor Frank Abu, Senior Pastor at The Redeemed Christian Church of God Living Word Liberation Centre, Southampton, thank you for sharing your insightful views.

To my pastor Rev Sandra Litchmore whose vibrancy for spiritual matters and leadership qualities have greatly impacted my life.

To my son-in-law Mr Opeoluwa Adekoye, my gratitude for your constant support and encouragement.

To many others whose names I am unable to mention, may the LORD reward the work of your hands and ministries in Jesus' Name, Amen.

And the Lord God said,
"It is not good that man should be alone; I will make him a helper comparable to him."

(Genesis 2:18)

Introduction

Since God created and designed the marriage institution, He sets out to honour marriages. Couples are strongly advised to remain faithful to one another so they can receive the blessings attached to the marriage covenant (Hebrews 13:4).

You might be wondering why I have chosen to write on the institution of marriage when marriages today are more slandered than celebrated. The reason is that God holds marriage in high esteem because it is part of His Divine agenda for humanity.

In Genesis 1:27-28, God created human beings in His likeness and image, male and female He created them.

> *Then God blessed them, and God said to them, "Be fruitful and multiply; fill the earth and subdue it; have dominion over the fish of the sea, over the birds of the air, and over every living thing that moves on the earth."*

However, this fruitfulness is only possible when there is a union between a man and a woman. That was how the institution of marriage came about in Genesis 2:18-20. The Lord God made the first woman from the first man Adam's rib and brought her to him.

God's desire was to fill the earth with His glory and reflected this by creating human beings. Marriage is one of God's great benevolences to mankind when you consider its benefit to individuals, homes and society at large. Alongside this are the benefits of parents imparting good home training and good morals to their children. These in turn impact the society resulting in healthy relationships overall.

Let us further consider the benefit of companionship that is desired by every partner in a marriage. *Two are better than one, because they have a good reward for their labor. If either of them falls one can uplift the other, but woe to anyone who falls and has no one to help them up* (Ecclesiastes 4:9-10). Couples can also strengthen their relationship by sharing their unique wisdom and insight. These benefits of marriage give us a reason to give thanks to God who instigated it.

Marriage requires work and total reliance on God, obediently following His leading with patient endurance.

Together in this book we will uncover ways you can strengthen your marriage, the importance of learning from the experience of other married couples, the power of prayer and seeking wise counsel before committing to a life partner. Individuals can apply these insights as they reflect on various causes of marriage breakdown which may lead to divorce.

A deep desire for marriage to be popular in our modern society compelled me to write this book. There are many reasons many young people do not want to commit to the honorable institution of marriage, the most common being the numerous broken marriages witnessed in our current society. Many who want to enjoy the benefits of a married life are not willing to commit to the responsibilities attached to marriage.

I would encourage all who wish to marry to know that marriage is good as 1 Corinthians 7:9 directs us saying, *But if they cannot control themselves, they should marry, for it is better to marry than to burn with passion*. There is no benefit in looking at those who have experienced a broken marriage, thinking the same will happen to you.

Bear in mind that not all marriages end up in divorce despite what statistics suggest. The best course of action is to trust God to guide you on this journey because He owns the original Master plan.

Let all that you do be done in love.
(1 Corinthians 16:14)

Chapter One:
The Origin of Marriage

We need to redeem the image of the marriage institution in the world and reveal the true intention of God's original plan concerning marriage. Hebrews 13:4 tells us that marriage should be honored by all, and the marriage bed undefiled.

This book seeks to:

- Provide useful information on how to achieve a successful marriage and guidance for those aspiring to be married.
- Offer advice, help and hope for couples experiencing breakdown in their marital homes.

Marriage was God's idea for mankind from the beginning. It began in the Garden of Eden when God saw that it was not good for man to be alone. God caused a deep sleep to fall on Adam, the first man He created. While Adam slept, God took a rib from his side and made a woman. The full story can be found in Genesis Chapter 2:15-25 below.

Genesis 2:15-25 (NKJV)

Then the Lord God took the man and put him in the garden of Eden to tend and keep it. And the Lord God commanded the man, saying, *"Of every tree of the garden you may freely eat; but of the tree of the knowledge of good and evil you shall not eat, for in the day that you eat of it you shall surely die."*

And the Lord God said, *"It is not good that man should be alone; I will make him a helper comparable to him."* Out of the ground the Lord God formed every beast of the field and every bird of the air, and brought them to Adam to see what he would call them. And whatever Adam called each living creature, that was its name. So Adam gave names to all cattle, to the birds of the air, and to every beast of the field. But for Adam there was not found a helper comparable to him.

And the Lord God caused a deep sleep to fall on Adam, and he slept; and He took one of his ribs, and closed up the flesh in its place. Then the rib which the Lord God had taken from man He made into a woman, and He brought her to the man. And Adam said: *"This is now bone of my bones and flesh of my flesh; she shall be called Woman, because she was taken out of Man."*

Therefore a man shall leave his father and mother and be joined to his wife, and they shall become one flesh. And they were both naked, the man and his wife, and were not ashamed.

This story is essential because it shows how much a man needs his rib, a woman like himself, someone to compliment and complete him. Sometimes this can be daunting, but with God's help all things are possible. The Owner's Manual, the Bible, gives clear instructions on how these points can be emphasized.

Adam was given authority to rule over all God's creation and quickly resumed his duty. God saw that it was not good for man to be alone. He put Adam to sleep and made the woman from Adam's rib, thereby creating a suitable help mate. The first couple Adam and Eve thereby established the institution of marriage, fulfilling God's desire.

We can therefore conclude that marriage is not an original idea from any government or nation. God knows how to create successful marriages since it is His original idea.

The following principles are meaningful within the institution of marriage:

- Marriage is Good
- Marriage is Honorable
- Marriage is Beneficial

- Marriage is Partnership
- Marriage is Union
- Marriage is Strength

Your ability to experience the above principles will depend on whether you have grasped the true meaning of marriage.

How then is this possible? The answer to this question is simple: consult the Visioner – God of all creation.

Time to reflect:
What is your current understanding of marriage?

What do you believe is the role of the **husband**?

What is the **wife's** role?

What is your **joint** role?

Name **five ways you can work in partnership** with your spouse to strengthen your marriage.

But from the beginning of the creation, God 'made them male and female.' 'For this reason a man shall leave his father and mother and be joined to his wife, and the two shall become one flesh'; so then they are no longer two, but one flesh. Therefore what God has joined together, let not man separate."
(Mark 10:6-9)

Chapter Two:
God's Purpose for Marriage

Therefore a man shall leave his father and
his mother and hold fast to his wife, and they
shall become one flesh.
(Genesis 2:24)

Marriage is instituted for three main purposes:

Companionship: Companionship releases help and comfort from each other within the relationship.

Protection from the sin of immorality: Helps to keep the marriage bed pure and undefiled.

Reproduction of young ones: God's commandment to the first man and woman was to be fruitful and multiply and replenish the Earth (Genesis 1:28).

How can you get your own rib? This question can be answered with certainty from God's Word. Proverbs 18:22 tells us that *He who finds a wife finds a good thing, and obtains favor from the LORD.* Further, if we acknowledge Him in all our ways, He will certainly direct our path (Proverbs 3:6). However, there are different stages of growth before the Altar of Marriage can be fully accessed.

Preparation for growth in maturity

This really starts from conception going into childhood, then supported during adulthood from parents, caretakers or mentors. One way of establishing this stage is by praying and meditating for your children about marriage starting from their earliest years. This aspect of meditation was seen in the case where Isaac went to the field to meditate in Genesis 24:63.

And Isaac went out to meditate in the field in the evening; and he lifted his eyes and looked, and there, the camels were coming.

Read the full account in Genesis chapter 24 which records how Abraham interceded for a wife for his son Isaac. God answered his prayers and provided a wife from Abraham's own people.

The preparation stage requires:

Physical maturity: A wife is expected to have become a woman, not remaining a girl, being free from the apron of her mother. On the other hand, a man leaves his parents' home to live an independent life when he is fully grown.

Emotional maturity: Couples going into the institution of marriage need to be emotionally mature, having adult traits. This will include being selfless and long suffering, not easily angered, and exercising patience. An emotionally mature person is stable against every tide of life.

Spiritual maturity: Couples must prove that they are mature in spirit, soul, and body (3 John v 2). Christ must be fully formed in them. This can only be achieved by knowing Christ as their personal Lord and Savior and living a sound Christian life. Marriage beautifies a life.

It is likened to finding a missing piece of an important puzzle when you desire to marry. ONLY God can put the puzzle together as you pray with patient expectation for every perfect gift comes from above (James 1:17).

It is also acceptable if you do not desire marriage but prefer to remain single which gives you more time to serve God and look after yourself. Whatever your preference, do it wholeheartedly as unto the Lord (Colossians 3:23). However, if you want to marry, this is GOOD NEWS, so please listen to me as I have a word from the LORD for you.

Marriage creates more joy and fulfilment in life, while working together as a couple eases the workload. Yet all these benefits can only happen with the help of the Holy Spirit.

Time to reflect:

Are you married? Answer these questions based on your personal experience. If you are not yet married, reflect on the emotional and spiritual qualities of your future spouse.

What examples of *emotional maturity* do you recognize...
- In yourself?

- In your spouse?

What examples of *spiritual maturity* do you recognize...
- In yourself?

- In your spouse?

If you are married: Can you name 3 tangible examples of God's favour upon your marriage?

Every good gift and every perfect gift is from above, and comes down from the Father of lights, with whom there is no variation or shadow of turning.
(James 1:17)

Chapter Three:
Creating a Successful Marriage

Since it is usually during the youth phase that one chooses a life partner, it is very important to be converted into Christianity early, so that your life can be guided by the Holy Spirit. A very common question frequently asked by singles who are intending to marry is *How do I know who God has destined for me?*

I admit that sometimes it is very difficult to know who your destined life partner is. However, the Bible is practical with God's promise in Proverbs 3: 5-6 to *Trust in the Lord*.

Some people blame God after marriage when things are not working well in their relationship as they reflect on various nourishing religious acts of service. Have you heard the following comments from puzzled believers? *I sing in church*; or *I am a Sunday school teacher: why is my marriage not working?*

One can do all those things and yet not have a heart that is consecrated to God. For this reason, it is good practice to regularly check your heart's status.

- *Are you sure that you have left your all on the altar?*

- *Can you confirm that you have not kept Christ out of certain parts of your life?*

- *Are you certain that you have not given the devil a foothold?*

If a marriage is from God, it is wonderful how two people can complement each other, even if they have completely different temperaments. On the other hand, there are those who will never round off each other because their natures are completely incompatible.

Such couples might stay together for years yet not blend. If they take an honest look at their relationship, they will notice that their marriage is spent fighting or surviving strife after strife.

It is essential to have the same interests in life with your partner. Having similar values, morals and aspirations will serve as a point of agreement and bonding. To LOVE means that both parties are headed in the same direction.

Read the following Scriptures in Genesis 2:18-24 and 2 Corinthians 6:14-16.as you prepare for the upcoming self-reflection.

And the Lord God said, *"It is not good that man should be alone; I will make him a helper comparable to him."* Out of the ground the Lord God formed every beast of the field and every bird of the air, and brought them to Adam to see what he would call them. And whatever Adam called each living creature, that was its name. So Adam gave names to all cattle, to the birds of the air, and to every beast of the field. But for Adam there was not found a helper comparable to him. And the Lord God caused a deep sleep to fall on Adam, and he slept; and He took one of his ribs, and closed up the flesh in its place. Then the rib which the Lord God had taken from man He made into a woman, and He brought her to the man. And Adam said: *"This is now bone of my bones and flesh of my flesh; she shall be called Woman, because she was taken out of Man."* Therefore a man shall leave his father and mother and be joined to his wife, and they shall become one flesh.

(Genesis 2:18-24)

Do not be unequally yoked together with unbelievers. For what fellowship has righteousness with lawlessness? And what communion has light with darkness? And what accord has Christ with Belial? Or what part has a believer with an unbeliever? And what agreement has the temple of God with idols? For you are the temple of the living God. As God has said: *"I will dwell in them and walk among them. I will be their God, and they shall be My people."*

(2 Corinthians 6:14-16)

Take the following quiz and reflect on where you stand on your spiritual and marital journey. Have your Bible to hand as you read through the relevant Scriptures. For your convenience I have also attached the reflection passages above.

Marriage Quiz!!

Who wants to get married?

Let us go through these questions together.

Q1: *What has my faith got to do with my love affairs?*

Answer: Found in 2 Corinthians 6:14-16.

Q2: *Is flirting wrong or sinful, or is it just a way of getting to know each other and showing interest?*

Answer: Your body is the temple of God; you are special.

Q3. *Is love at first sight a real thing? Is it possible? Are there any dangers to it?*

Answer: This is when you fall in love with someone the very first time you see them without knowing who they are. It does happen! The danger lies in committing to each other before knowing if you are compatible.

Q4. *To what extent does what I watch, listen to, and read influence my view of love and the kind of relationship I pursue?*

Answer: What you allow into your mind through the gates of your eyes and ears, forms your thoughts which eventually shape your decisions and actions.

Indulging in watching immoral films or reading illicit books and magazines will compromise your judgment about love, mostly giving you a false reality of such a beautiful thing.

Q5. *Is what I wear and do really that important? Does the status of my heart matter? What does God look at? Does that sound familiar? Is how you talk, dress, or carry yourself of any relevance in positioning yourself for the true love Christ has orchestrated for you?*

Answer: Paul admonishes Timothy a young man to be an example of a believer of Jesus Christ in conduct and behaviour. The same is true for you.

Q6. *Have you identified how God speaks to you?*

Answer: God is a Spirit; He speaks to our spirit inwardly. This can be expressed through:

1. *Inward conviction or persuasion*
2. *Confidence and peace*
3. *Lack of peace or unsettlement denoting NO*
4. *Dreams and visions*
5. *A Bible verse literally leaping up to you on an issue*
6. *Circumstances not supporting your decisions*

7. *A Confirmer*. God can bring someone who knows nothing about you to say a word that will confirm your decision.

I will further advise that you should have a mature Christian mentor to check things with, in the same manner that Eli helped the young prophet Samuel to ascertain the voice of God (Ministry of Eli).

Time to reflect:

How does God speak to you?
Name 3 instructions God gave you in the past.

How did you react? (Did you follow through or delay due to fear or doubt?

Mention three results of your obedience and give thanks.

God directs our paths every day. Learn to discern the Voice of God as you meditate on His Word and spend time in prayer.

Let us pray:

Search me, O God, and know my heart; try me, and know my anxieties; and see if there is any wicked way in me, and lead me in the way everlasting.

(Psalm 139:23-24)

Chapter Four:
Three Pillars of Marriage

Every marriage is built on a foundation and held by pillars. What determines the stability of that marriage and therefore its success in lasting well, is the kind of foundation and pillars in place to hold it up. In this section we will walk through the three pillars I believe are crucial to nurturing a successful and stable marriage.

1ˢᵗ *Pillar: Your identity*

Part of the process of spiritual formation involves developing a sense of identity. Our spirits are formed as we embrace who we truly are and the deepest truth about any person is hidden in his or her identity.

Who am I? This is the cry of the young people.

Non-Christians have no resources except the surrounding world to define their identity. Your parents, teachers, friends, and other people form a kind of mirror which reflects your self-image. However, it is possible you still don't know who you are.

So, *who are YOU?*

A Christian is one who has been transformed by the life of Jesus through His death and resurrection. This transformation can be likened to a caterpillar becoming a butterfly so beautiful and radiant. Having been baptized into Christ's death, we are united with Him in His resurrection and therefore enabled to walk in newness of life (Romans 6:1-4). According to 1ˢᵗ John 2:14b you are strong, the Word of God abides in you and you have overcome the wicked one. That is who you are.

Many of the problems young people experience come from lack of a solid identity. Many are uncertain of who they are. With their rapidly changing physical bodies under flurry of hormones, and confused by the changing opinions of others, these youngsters live in a turbulent inner world.

This causes emotional stress and confusion. They desire to feel loved and wanted and may end up giving in to sexual exploitation, promiscuity, and other immoral acts. The result is frustration, unhappiness, and further confusion of identity.

On the other hand, Christian youth who are united with Christ in His death and resurrection are enabled to live a new life above these stresses.

Youth who do not know their identity, constantly measure themselves against others as a means of establishing their worth. This is a losing game as there will always be another person more handsome, smarter, or funnier. To know who you are in Christ is to rise above the comparison and pressures of life. This is done through the redemptive work of Jesus Christ.

You are valuable, hence Christ died for you. Grow in your relationship with God as you commit to daily reading the Bible and prayerfully meditating on the Scriptures. Create a lifestyle of attending church regularly to fellowship with other likeminded people which will further cement your identity and help you in those wavering times.

2nd *Pillar: Your literature*

Your eyes are an important gateway to your life. It therefore comes as no surprise that reading and being exposed to some of the content found in certain newspapers, magazines and books shape and form your belief system. You may find that some of these offline and online forums, media outlets and adverts are impregnated with flirtatious talk, playboy innuendos, impurity, and adulterous stories.

Some stories may run along these lines:

A married man and a young girl fall in love with each other, or a married man starts an illicit relationship with another man's wife, or a young man meets a married woman.

The aim of such books, novels and contents whether as a hard or soft copy is simply to defile you, making it harder to live a life that is worthwhile. Such stories are often written with an aim to captivate you and keep you wanting more of that theme. The hidden agenda seeks to weaken the foundation and pillars for which you later build a marriage. Be careful what you read, the programs, documentaries, films, and social media posts you spend your time enjoying. They can either make you or break you.

3rd Pillar: Your conduct and wardrobe (while single)

Nothing is more beautiful than a happy, friendly, laughing, easy to get along person with a good sense of humour. If you are aspiring to get married, develop these traits, they make you even more attractive than outward clothing, physique, or makeup. Be nice and helpful too.

Let your speech be sweet and not too loud, avoid swearing. Do not be a liar; it puts people off and leads to your words becoming untrustworthy.

Whether you sit or stand, keep your body well, stay poised and always look well-presented. Dress moderately and avoid wearing revealing clothes which can put people off. This is especially important for self-respecting women who want to attract the right kind of man. Simply put, dress how you want to be addressed. Read 1st Timothy 2:9-10:

In like manner also, that the women adorn themselves in modest apparel, with propriety and moderation, not with braided hair or gold or pearls or costly clothing, but, which is proper for women professing godliness, with good works.

Another consideration to be careful about is falling in love at first sight. You are advised to seek God's will before entering any relationship. There is wisdom in getting to know the person before committing to building a deeper relationship.

The Book of Judges chapter 16 relates the story of a Philistine giant named Samson who fell in love with a woman of the world named Delilah. Later she deceived him into revealing the secret of his God-given strength after which she sold Samson to his enemies at a great price (they gouged his eyes out). Samson thought he had found the love of his life, only to be duped by the woman he trusted. That was an ill-suited union.

Getting too close to someone before learning about their history, beliefs and lifestyle can lead to undesired problems. Suitors might later find it harder to disentangle from such negative relationships.

Some individuals seek the friendship of someone they perceive to be well-to-do. However, after the couple tie the knot, the partner reveals their true colours and starts to oppress the spouse who regrets his decision.

Being unequally yoked with someone can have devastating results which are avoidable when one follows the advice in this book.

Time to reflect:
If you are not yet married...
How will you apply each of the 3 pillars as you prepare for marriage?

As a married person...
What advice would you give a friend who is looking to get married, or a newlywed couple?

Chapter Five:
Five Benefits of Marriage

Marriage is beautiful, so don't allow anyone to discourage you based on their own negative experience or story. We know now that God created the institution of marriage. We also know that He saw everything He created to be good. Therefore, it is safe to say that marriage is good and there are worthwhile benefits to marrying according to God's will for you. Below are five benefits of a godly marriage:

Benefit One. A good marriage gives companionship because when two people who love each get married, there is peace, joy and a sense of fulfilment.

Benefit Two. The altar of marriage protects against sexual immorality because God's idea of sex is to be within the confines of marriage, as 1 Corinthians 7:2 revels: *Nevertheless, because of sexual immorality, let each man have his own wife, and let each woman have her own husband.*

God hates all forms of sexual perversion including adultery and fornication. He is the righteous Judge who will judge such immoral conduct according to His Word. (Hebrews 13:4).

Benefit Three. A good marriage is like a small church. When a couple unites to serve God and pray together in agreement, God will not fail to answer their prayers.

Benefit Four. A good marriage brings prosperity when both partners are operating in the blessing of God. They will be correctly guided to make good decisions as they look to Him.

Benefit Five. A good marriage will raise godly children, lead to vibrant churches and a peaceful society. Statistics show that children from broken homes find it more difficult to cope with life issues. It is therefore worth fighting for the destiny of your children and for the stability of your home.

Since the devil is in a rage against the marriage institution couples need to fight the good fight of faith and pray constantly for their homes.

Time to reflect:

If you are married:
Name five benefits you are enjoying in your marriage.
(*If you are single or aspiring to tie the knot*, name 5 benefits you want to manifest in your marriage).

What additional benefits will you ask God to bless you with looking ahead?

Submitting to one another in
the fear of God.
(Ephesians 5:21)

Chapter Six:
Challenges Within Marriages

The title of this chapter may come as a surprise to you because all you have known so far are the fairy-tale joys of marriage. Whilst I don't want to seem like the bearer of negativity, my aim is to equip you with realistic insight so you will be informed and know how to deal with these issues should you encounter them in your marriage.

At this point it is important for you to realise that just as no person is spared of problems in life, no marriage is void of challenges. Your ability to overcome them rests on how prepared you are prior to entering this beautiful phase of your life. You will understand God's purpose and will for marriages which we have explored in previous chapters.

I would like to offer advice and hope for couples experiencing breakdowns in their marriage. God knows and cares about what you are going through. He is the Invincible God Almighty who can turn things around in your favour.

Rest assured that what God cannot do or cannot change does not exist. Look to Him once more and experience His mighty power as you pray.

It is no secret that the devil hates marriages because God ordained it; the enemy is against anything God approves. The devil also knows there are great benefits to being married. For example, it is well recognised that two are better than one and they will surely be rewarded for their labour.

Additionally, marriage resembles a small church in that whatever a husband and wife agree upon in line with God's Word, it will happen through the prayer of agreement. (Matthew 18:19). We will now look at some possible issues that may arise in marriage.

Challenge One: Differences in personality

No two individuals are the same people, not even twins. Therefore, do not be discouraged to discover differences between you and your partner as you progress in your marriage.

It is not unusual for newlyweds to experience some initial friction as they try to blend after the 'honeymoon' period. This stems from the fact that you are two individuals coming from two different backgrounds and upbringing, with varying experiences that have shaped and formed the pillars that guide and guard that partner in the marriage.

So how is this dealt with? The answer is PATIENCE. Know this and know peace. Married couples need to be patient with each other as they begin to settle into their new life together.

It takes time to get to truly know a person and you cannot fully do this during courtship. You may be thinking *we will just date for longer*. However, once you get married expect to discover new things on a regular basis.

COMMUNICATION is another key to dealing with this issue. Discovering something new in a spouse does not mean they have changed; it may just be that you were not fully aware of that person's trait. If the new discovery matters to you, bring it up. Have a discussion to gain perspective so you can decide to either accept it, pray about it, or adjust.

Challenge Two: Issues with in-laws

There are two categories of people in this area. The first refers to the person reading this whose mind is filled with pleasant thoughts and smiles about their in-laws. The second type of person suddenly has a flurry of thoughts reminding them of the need to focus on this section.

Whichever category you are in, it can be a very challenging task trying to understand and relate with your in-laws whether now or in the future. This may be because of cultural differences which can escalate to problems if not handled appropriately.

The solution to this rests on two things: praying for WISDOM and accepting that your in-laws are the people that gave birth to or brought up your spouse, for which they deserve some respect and appreciation. Let your husband or wife know how you feel about something that his or her family has done or how they made you feel. This requires wisdom. Communicating your concerns is important if you want to see change in that area.

Challenge Three: Lack of finances

Money is good. It comes as no surprise then that lack of money within the home can cause friction whether the shortage is caused by reduced inflow, poor management, or no income. The situation can escalate especially if it is felt to be one-sided, or worst-case scenarios are not discussed beforehand.

I encourage all intending couples to engage in talking about all aspects of money before marriage. Be aware that when you become one in marriage, money issues do not suddenly disappear. While talking about it does not instantly become easier, if the awkwardness around such a sensitive topic has been broken, which is usually half the issue, you have a good start.

Challenge Four: Delay in the promise of having children

Married couples have already been blessed by God to be fruitful and have godly children. In Genesis 1:28 God commanded us to be fruitful, multiply and replenish the earth. Delay in childbearing within a married couple has the potential to create tension, bring about doubt and cause problems if they are not aware of the brokenness that may result from the inability to conceive.

Sometimes there are external pressures, career pressures, personal timelines and many more factors that contribute to the brokenness that can arise from delay in childbearing.

My advice to couples in such circumstances is to trust God and wait upon Him as they pray together for godly children. Togetherness and oneness on this issue is stronger than any personal determination one individual may have. You can become each other's backbones when the overwhelming feelings come flooding in.

Secondly, do not be too spiritual to seek medical advice; even the Bible tells us that "*My people perish for lack of knowledge*" (Hosea 4:6). Seeking professional or medical help does not negate your belief in God, it is applying simple wisdom.

Lastly, be expectant because God cannot fail. Based on all the issues we have discussed above, we cannot be ignorant of the devil's devices. As believers we must be aware that the enemy (the devil) is against marriages.

The origin of marital challenges can often be attributed to Satanic assaults. Be vigilant, know who you are in Christ and guard your marriage with prayers. Pray as an individual but do not ignore the place of praying with your husband or wife; this carries a different kind of covering.

Time to reflect:

What challenges have you experienced/do you foresee in your marriage?

If you are married: What solutions have helped your marriage to grow?

Based on your personal experience, what advice would you offer a newlywed couple on how to manage the following challenges?
Personality differences?

Finance?

In-laws?

Delay in having children?

Prayers for Singles

It is important to ask God what you need and desire as you prepare for marriage since He knows what is best for you. Use the following prayers and add your own.

1. Jeremiah 29:11 - *For I know the thoughts that I think toward you, says the Lord, thoughts of peace and not of evil, to give you a future and a hope.*

Prayer: I thank the Lord for the good and perfect plans He has for me.

2. Philippians 1:10 - *that you may approve the things that are excellent, that you may be sincere and without offense till the day of Christ,*

Prayer: I pray that God would grant me the desire to be sincere and want to do His will in every situation.

3. Matthew 6:33 - *But seek first the kingdom of God and His righteousness, and all these things shall be added to you.*

Prayer: I pray that I will faithfully serve God using my talents and gifting for His glory, in Jesus' Mighty Name.

4. 1 Timothy 6:6 - *Now godliness with contentment is great gain.*

Prayer: I pray that God will help me to be content in every situation.

5. 2 Corinthians 5:7 - *For we walk by faith, not by sight.*

Reflection: Tell the Lord about your desire to walk by faith and not by sight.

6. Isaiah 40:29 - *He gives power to the weak, and to those who have no might He increases strength.*

Reflection: Admit your struggles in choosing a marriage partner and ask God to help you submit to His good will.

7. Matthew 7:7 - *"Ask, and it will be given to you; seek, and you will find; knock, and it will be opened to you."*

Prayer: LORD, I thank You for answering my prayers.

As you daily make your requests to the LORD, you will begin to see your prayers being answered. Remember to give thanks for every answered prayer.

Chapter Seven:
Marriage Advice

By the grace of God alone, my husband and I have been married now for over 36 years. I will leave you with some useful advice gained from years of counselling couples in navigating the marriage institution.

- Do not be ignorant of the devil's devices and tactics. Be smart and always look out for your home.

- Develop yourself through regular Bible study, prayers, attending church and marriage seminars, and reading Christian books.

- Do not quit when there is a problem. Instead, seek counsel from a professional marriage counsellor who is trained and well-equipped to advice on marriage from a biblical perspective. You can also seek support from loved ones in a timely manner.

- Do not leave problems to escalate beyond resolution. Never surrender your marriage to the devil. Resist him and continue to pray without ceasing because God brought you together to bless you. Be resilient and never give up on what God has joined together.

- Recognize that marriage requires active participation, patience and endurance fueled by consistent prayer to grow and keep the flame of harmonious love alive.

How can one strengthen their mindset and expectations leading up to marriage?

- Seek wise counsel at the earliest opportunity before knowing who to marry. Do not wait until a few weeks before your wedding day to sign up for a counselling course aimed at gaining valuable knowledge and support towards your desire to get married.

- Attend retreats for Christian singles to establish relationships with other like-minded single individuals.

- It is important to move forward with a healthy mindset when searching for a spouse. Consider holding private talks with people who have been married for a long time; allow them to share their experiences with you.

- Read the Word of God. Studying Scriptures on marriage will help you identify if the counselling provided aligns with God's Word.

- Another way of helping those seeking to get married is for Churches to include talks on marriages in their conferences and conventions. This should not be left for youth conferences alone.

- Prayerful men and women should intercede ahead of their children's marriages and teach them about marriage while they are still living at home. Make time to have these conversations when your children ask for advice. Our society is made up of children from various homes. *If the foundations are destroyed, what can the righteous do*? (Psalm 11:3). Our responsibility as parents and nurturers is to start praying for our children while they are young, before they start thinking about marriage.

- During the Covid-19 pandemic we learned that a wedding does not need to be elaborate to make it sweet. Planning your wedding in line with your available budget will help you avoid starting your marriage with financial debt which can easily create unnecessary strain on a couple's relationship.

Having a desire to get married is a wonderful thing. I would therefore encourage you to take the bold step forward but seek God's will before doing so.

Beware of the present-day teachings on equality of rights as this may cause friction in the home if not applied wisely.

1. The **husband** is the head of the home; he is to love his wife as Christ loves the church.

2. The **wife** should submit to her husband as the church submits to Christ. She should not be treated as a slave, but as a lover.

3. **Both partners** should submit to one another in the fear of the Lord and wash each other's hands. (Read Ephesians 5:25-33 on the following page for deeper insight).

I pray every rage of the enemy against our homes is dismantled in Jesus' mighty Name. Amen.

Husbands, love your wives, just as Christ also loved the church and gave Himself for her, that He might sanctify and cleanse her with the washing of water by the word, that He might present her to Himself a glorious church, not having spot or wrinkle or any such thing, but that she should be holy and without blemish.

So husbands ought to love their own wives as their own bodies; he who loves his wife loves himself. For no one ever hated his own flesh, but nourishes and cherishes it, just as the Lord does the church.

For we are members of His body, of His flesh and of His bones. *"For this reason a man shall leave his father and mother and be joined to his wife, and the two shall become one flesh."*

This is a great mystery, but I speak concerning Christ and the church. Nevertheless let each one of you in particular so love his own wife as himself, and let the wife see that she respects her husband.

(Ephesians 5:25-33)

Time to reflect:

From your experience growing up, **what was the relationship between your parents?**

How does your memory compare with your own experience with your spouse?

Name *four things* you will do more of/start doing as a couple going forward.

Chapter Eight:
Redemption in Christ

He has delivered us from the power of darkness and conveyed us into the kingdom of the Son of His love, in whom we have redemption through His blood, the forgiveness of sins.

(Colossians 1:13-14)

What is Redemption?

Redemption involves:

- Making up for the fault of others
- Fulfilling a promise
- Paying a debt
- Regaining possession of something in exchange for payment
- Being saved from sin or evil

Jesus Christ did all this for mankind through His death and glorious resurrection. For we have all sinned and fallen short of God's kindness and glory (Romans 3:23). The best among us have done wrong things and behaved badly at some point in our lives. Jesus paid the price of our redemption by giving His life for us on the cross (Matthew 27:50).

Scripture further explains that the kingdom of heaven is like a certain king who made a marriage feast for his son and sent out servants to remind those who were invited to the wedding banquet. However, the guests did not attend. You can read the full account in Matthew 22:1-10.

In this book we have been discussing marriage and its benefits, hence the need to thank God. However, another wedding is coming when we leave this world and go to meet our loving Creator in heaven. For there is another life after this mortal life; this earth is not the end of all things.

The heavenly wedding is called *The Marriage of the Lamb* which is the consummation of our union with the Lord Jesus Christ.

Revelation 19:7 records, *"Let us be glad and rejoice and give Him glory, for the marriage of the Lamb has come, and His wife (bride) has made herself ready."*

To be qualified into this glorious marriage ceremony, we must accept God's invitation and allow Jesus Christ to be our personal Lord and Saviour while we dwell on Earth. It is simple because Jesus paid it all on the cross when He died for us all. Our side of the deal is to believe and agree that Christ did that for us and accept His invitation into our heart by faith. Yes, it really is that simple!

Would you like to take part in this *Marriage of the Lamb* after your time here on Earth? What an exciting decision! I couldn't be prouder of this bold step that is about to change the course of your life.

The first step is to accept God's invitation now. Give your heart to Him through faith by repeating this prayer with a sincere heart:

Lord Jesus Christ,
I believe You died for me on the cross.
I believe You rose again from the dead and
You are alive for evermore.
Please forgive all my sins as I repent today.
Cleanse me with Your blood.
Come into my heart today as my personal
Lord and Saviour.
In Jesus' Name, Amen.

If you have just said this prayer, you have become a child of God. *Hallelujah*!!!

Join a Bible believing church and grow in faith.

Please drop me an email at fol58@outlook.com and let me know how I can be praying for you.

Testimony, Prayer, Thanksgiving Time

Share your testimony of how the LORD has transformed your life as you read this book and followed through with the reflections and action steps.

Write a short prayer of thanksgiving for everything you have called forth by faith as you grow in your marriage and family relationships.

Thank you for allowing me into your space to help you achieve your breakthroughs.

Please drop me an email at *fol58@outlook.com* and let me know how I can be praying for you. God bless you.

Gratefully in Christ's service,

Min Margaret Odeleye

About the Author

Margaret Olufolake Odeleye surrendered her life to Jesus Christ and accepted Him as her LORD and Saviour at the tender age of 14.

Following Christ's leading in her life, she came to England over 2 decades ago as a Registered Nurse.

Margaret attended *Jubilee Life Ministry Bible College* in Hersham, England, and completed her Clergy Training in 2003. This experience has hugely impacted her life.

Margaret is a lay minister in the *New Testament Church of God* with a passion for evangelism and outreach.

She is married to a solicitor who shares her passion for evangelism; they are blessed with 3 adult children.

Follow the Author on Amazon:

https://www.amazon.co.uk/Margaret-Odeleye/e/B0984R47TW/

Other Books by the Author

GET YOUR COPY TODAY!

Debt of Gratitude

Margaret Odeleye

Available from Amazon at...
https://tinyurl.com/DebtOfGratitudeUK

https://www.amazon.co.uk/Margaret-Odeleye/e/B0984R47TW/